P9-CSW-739

SAY UNCLE

ALSO BY KAY RYAN

Elephant Rocks

Flamingo Watching

Strangely Marked Metal

Dragon Acts to Dragon Ends

SAY UNCLE

poems

by
KAY RYAN

GROVE PRESS • NEW YORK

Published simultaneously in Canada
Printed in the United States of America

Library of Congress Cataloging-in-Publication Data

Ryan, Kay.
  Say Uncle : poems / by Kay Ryan.
    p. cm.
ISBN-10: 0-8021-3717-2
ISBN-13: 978-0-8021-3717-3
    I. Title
PS3568.Y38 S29 2000
811'.54—dc21   00-026454

Design by Julie Duquet

Grove Press
an imprint of Grove/Atlantic, Inc.
841 Broadway
New York, NY 10003

Distributed by Publishers Group West

www.groveatlantic.com

08 09 10 11 12   10 9 8 7 6 5 4 3

ACKNOWLEDGMENTS

Grateful acknowledgment is made to the following publications in which these poems first appeared:

THE ATLANTIC MONTHLY: *Among English Verbs;* COLUMBIA: *Weakness and Doubt, Drops in the Bucket, Failure 2, Gaps, Your Face Will Stick, Silence Islands, The Museum of False Starts, Agreement;* THE GEORGIA REVIEW: *Waste;* THE JOURNAL: *Help, Gravity;* THE NEW YORKER: *Blandeur, The Excluded Animals, The Old Cosmologists, Yeses, Failure, Deferred Silence, A Hundred Bolts of Satin, Patience, Crown, The Job;* THE PARIS REVIEW: *Crash, Lime Light, Dutch, Matrigupta;* PARNASSUS: *Forgetting;* PARTISAN REVIEW: *Death by Fruit;* PLOUGHSHARES: *Corners, Mockingbird;* POETRY: *Grazing Horses, Don't Look Back, Herring, The Pieces That Fall to Earth, Winter Fear, Why We Must Struggle, The Fabric of Life, Test, Two More and Up Goes the Donkey;* THE RECORDER: *Bad Day;* SALON: *Nothing Ventured;* SOLO: *Ticket;* THE SOUTHERN REVIEW: *Water under the Bridge, Beasts, Composition, Diamonds, Coming and Going, Say Uncle, It's Always Darkest Just before the Dawn, Great Thoughts;* THE THREEPENNY REVIEW: *Chemise, Cheshire;* THE YALE REVIEW: *That Will to Divest, The Catch, The Pass;* WATER/STONE: *Blunt;* ZYZZYVA: *Star Block*

"That Will to Divest" also appeared in THE BEST AMERICAN POETRY 1999 (Scribner, 1999). "Angles of Sun" appeared in LIGHTHOUSE POEMS (Thornwillow Press, 2000). "Patience" was reprinted in the pamphlet series "Poems in the Waiting Room" by the Poetry Club of the City Literary Institute of London.

Some of these poems have appeared in an Aralia Press fine press edition, *That Will to Divest,* 1999.

For Carol

CONTENTS

SAY UNCLE

SAY UNCLE

Every day
you say,
*Just one
more try.*
Then another
irrecoverable
day slips by.
You will
say *ankle,*
you will
say *knuckle;*
why won't
you why
won't you
say *uncle?*

CORNERS

All but saints
and hermits
mean to paint
themselves
toward an exit

leaving a
pleasant ocean
of azure or jonquil
ending neatly
at the doorsill.

But sometimes
something happens:

a minor dislocation
by which the doors
and windows
undergo a
small rotation
to the left a little

—but repeatedly.
It isn't
obvious immediately.

Only toward evening
and from the
farthest corners
of the houses
of the painters

comes a chorus
of individual keening
as of kenneled dogs
someone is mistreating.

STAR BLOCK

There is no such thing
as *star block*.
We do not think of
locking out the light
of other galaxies.
It is light
so rinsed of impurities
(heat, for instance)
that it excites
no antibodies in us.
Yet people are
curiously soluble
in starlight.
Bathed in its
absence of insistence
their substance
loosens willingly,
their bright
designs dissolve.
Not proximity
but distance
burns us with love.

MOCKINGBIRD

Nothing whole
is so bold,
we sense. Nothing
not cracked is
so exact and
of a piece. He's
the distempered
emperor of parts,
the king of patch,
the master of
pastiche, who so
hashes other birds'
laments, so minces
their capriccios, that
the dazzle of dispatch
displaces the originals.
As though brio
really does beat feeling,
the way two aces
beat three hearts
when it's cards
you're dealing.

A Hundred Bolts of Satin

All you
have to lose
is one
connection
and the mind
uncouples
all the way back.
It seems
to have been
a train.
There seems
to have been
a track.
The things
that you
unpack
from the
abandoned cars
cannot sustain
life: a crate of
tractor axles,
for example,

a dozen dozen
clasp knives,
a hundred
bolts of satin—
perhaps you
specialized
more than
you imagined.

THE EXCLUDED ANIMALS

Only a certain
claque of beasts
is part of the
crèche racket

forming a
steamy-breathed
semicircle
around the
baby basket.

Anything more
exotic than
a camel
is out of luck
this season.

Not that the
excluded animals envy
the long-lashed
sycophants;

cormorants
don't toady,
nor do toads
adore anybody
for any reason.

Nor do the
unchosen alligators,
grinning their
three-foot grin
as they laze
in the blankety waters
like the blankets on Him.

Blandeur

If it please God,
let less happen.
Even out Earth's
rondure, flatten
Eiger, blanden
the Grand Canyon.
Make valleys
slightly higher,
widen fissures
to arable land,
remand your
terrible glaciers
and silence
their calving,
halving or doubling
all geographical features
toward the mean.
Unlean against our hearts.
Withdraw your grandeur
from these parts.

COMPOSITION

Language is a diluted aspect of matter.
—Joseph Brodsky

No. Not *diluted.*
Flaked; wafered;
but not watered.
Language is matter
leafing like a book
with the good taste
of rust and exposure
the way ironwork
petals near the coast.
But so many more
colors than rust:
or, argent, others—
a vast heraldic shield
of beautiful readable
fragments revealed
as Earth delaminates:
how the metals scatter,
how matter turns
animate.

PATIENCE

Patience is
wider than one
once envisioned,
with ribbons
of rivers
and distant
ranges and
tasks undertaken
and finished
with modest
relish by
natives in their
native dress.
Who would
have guessed
it possible
that waiting
is sustainable—
a place with
its own harvests.
Or that in
time's fullness

the diamonds
of patience
couldn't be
distinguished
from the genuine
in brilliance
or hardness.

COMING AND GOING

There is a
recently discovered
order, neither
sponges nor fishes,
which is never
at the mercy
of conditions.
If currents shift,
these fleshy zeppelins
can reverse directions
from inside—
their guts are
so easily modified.
Coming versus going
is therefore
not the crisis
it is for people,

who have to scramble
to keep anything
from showing
when we see
what we can't see
coming, going.

Nothing Ventured

Nothing exists as a block
and cannot be parceled up.
So if nothing's ventured
it's not just talk;
it's the big wager.
Don't you wonder
how people think
the banks of space
and time don't matter?
How they'll drain
the big tanks down to
slime and salamanders
and want thanks?

THAT WILL TO DIVEST

Action creates
a taste
for itself.
Meaning: once
you've swept
the shelves
of spoons
and plates
you kept
for guests,
it gets harder
not to also
simplify the larder,
not to dismiss
rooms, not to
divest yourself
of all the chairs
but one, not
to test what
singleness can bear,
once you've begun.

WINTER FEAR

Is it just winter
or is this worse.
Is this the year
when outer damp
obscures a deeper curse
that spring can't fix,
when gears that
turn the earth
won't shift the view,
when clouds won't lift
though all the skies
go blue.

GRAZING HORSES

Sometimes the
green pasture
of the mind
tilts abruptly.
The grazing horses
struggle crazily
for purchase
on the frictionless
nearly vertical
surface. Their
furniture-fine
legs buckle
on the incline,
unhorsed by slant
they weren't
designed to climb
and can't.

WASTE

Not even waste
is inviolate.
The day misspent,
the love misplaced,
has inside it
the seed of redemption.
Nothing is exempt
from resurrection.
It is tiresome
how the grass
re-ripens, greening
all along the punched
and mucked horizon
once the bison
have moved on,
leaning into hunger
and hard luck.

FORGETTING

Forgetting takes space.
Forgotten matters displace
as much anything else as
anything else. We must
skirt unlabeled crates
as though it made sense
and take them when we go
to other states.

THE FOURTH WISE MAN

The fourth wise man
disliked travel. If
you walk, there's the
gravel. If you ride,
there's the camel's attitude.
He far preferred
to be inside in solitude
to contemplate the star
that had been getting
so much larger
and more *prolate* lately—
stretching vertically
(like the souls of martyrs)
toward the poles
(or like the yawns of babies).

BEASTS

Time lingers
quietly in attics.
Romantics are
always fingering
some discolored
fabric or other,
feeling a deep
nostalgia for sepia,
a mellow sadness
at what keeps
but yellows.
But other people
don't trust ambering
or court the filigrees
of rust. They've
seen lost greens
of memory ignite,
dead dogs released,
and don't invite
the rainbow beasts.

GAPS

Gaps don't
just happen.
There is a
generative element
inside them,
a welling motion
as when cold
waters shoulder
up through
warmer oceans.
And where gaps
choose to widen,
coordinates warp,
even in places
constant since
the oldest maps.

THE FABRIC OF LIFE

It is very stretchy.
We know that, even if
many details remain
sketchy. It is complexly
woven. That much too
has pretty well been
proven. We are loath
to continue our lessons,
which consist of slaps
as sharp and dispersed
as bee stings from
a smashed nest,
when any strand snaps—
hurts working far past
the locus of rupture,
attacking threads
far beyond anything
we would have said
connects.

HELP

Imagine *help*
as a syllable,
awkward but utterable.

How would it work
and in which distress?
How would one gauge
the level of duress
at which to pitch
the plea? How bad
would something
have to be?

It's hard,
coming from a planet
where if we needed something
we had it.

AGREEMENT

The satisfactions
of agreement are
immediate as sugar—
a melting of the
granular, a syrup
that lingers, shared
not singular.
Many prefer it.

The Old Cosmologists

When their cosmology
grows soft and spongy
and unreal, the
old cosmologists
get touchy. They feel
they should have
held it off, they should
have known about it
in advance, they
should have stretched
the interstellar cloth
or sown a row of stars
along a rift just to the left
of Mars or guessed
about a pin-sized patch
of purple gas or grafted
comets tail-to-tail,
and thus or otherwise
suppressed the drift;

as if change were not
something that just happens
at certain stages
but a private test failed
moment by moment
as age is.

THE PASS

Even in climes
without snow
one cannot go
forward sometimes.
Things test you.
You are part of
the Donners or
part of the rescue:
a muleteer in
earflaps; a
formerly hearty
Midwestern farmer
perhaps. Both
parties trapped
within sight
of the pass.

THE PIECES THAT FALL TO EARTH

One could
almost wish
they wouldn't;
they are so
far apart,
so random.
One cannot
wait, cannot
abandon waiting.
The three or
four occasions
of their landing
never fade.
Should there
be more, there
will never be
enough to make
a pattern
that can equal
the commanding
way they matter.

Don't Look Back

This is not
a problem
for the neckless.
Fish cannot
recklessly
swivel their heads
to check
on their fry;
no one expects
this. They are
torpedoes of
disinterest,
compact capsules
that rely
on the odds
for survival,
unfollowed by
the exact and modest
number of goslings
the S-necked
goose is—

who if she
looks back
acknowledges losses
and if she does not
also loses.

IT'S ALWAYS DARKEST JUST
BEFORE THE DAWN

But how dark
is *darkest?*
Does it get
jet—or tar—
black; does it
glint and increase
in hardness
or turn viscous?
Are there stages
of darkness
and chips
to match against
its increments,
holding them
up to our blindness,
estimating when
we'll have the
night behind us?

BLUNT

If we could love
the blunt
and not
the point

we would
almost constantly
have what we want.

What is the
blunt of this
I would ask you

our conversation
weeding up
like the Sargasso.

DIAMONDS

Is the snail
sharpened
by crawling
over diamonds?
Is her foot
hardened
so it can't
carry her?
No. Snails
make mucus.
Even the
most precious
barriers
to lettuce
are useless.

HERRING

A thousand
tiny silver
thoughtlets
play in the mind,
untarnished
as herring.

They shutter
like blinds,
then sliver,
then utterly
vanish.

Is it unkind
to hope
some will
eat others;
is it uncaring?

THE MUSEUM OF FALSE STARTS

It is incredibly
beautiful but
unfinished—
actually hardly
more than imagined.
There are the beginnings
of a gallery of
ribbon-lovely thoughts
that vanish,
shadowy gardens
briefly visible
at shifting angles,
and, caught
in an ancient ash,
the single spiraling
horn of an otherwise
unfashioned animal.

The Silence Islands

These are the
Silence Islands,
where what outsiders
would consider
nearly imperceptible
aural amusements
land like coconuts
on the crystalline
hammers and anvils
of the native inhabitants.
Theirs is a refinement
so exquisite that,
for example, to rhyme
anything with *hibiscus*
is interdicted anytime
children or anyone weakened
by sickness is expected.

TICKET

This is the ticket
I failed to spend.
It is still in my pocket
at the fair's end.
It is not only
suffering or grief
or even boredom
of which we are
offered more than
enough.

Thief

Like a watch thief
fitted with secret pockets
he felt a downward tug
on his spring jacket.

Like spring grasses
harboring crickets
he emitted a suspicious
ticking racket.

All spring
he had the feeling
that he was the one
doing the stealing.

CHESHIRE

It's not the cat,
it's the smile that
lasts, toothy
and ruthless.
It's facts like this
we like to resist—
how our parts
may lack allegiance
to the whole;
how the bonds
may be more casual
than we know; how
much of us
might vanish
and how well
some separate part
might manage.

YESES

Just behind
the door,
a second.
But smaller
by a few inches.
Behind which
a third again
diminishes.
Then more
and more,
forming a
foreshortened
corridor or
niche of yeses
ending in
a mouse's
entrance
with a knob
too small
to pinch.

DEATH BY FRUIT

Only the crudest
of the *vanitas* set
ever thought
you *had* to get
a skull into the picture
whether you needed
its tallowy color
near the grapes
or not. Others,
stopping to consider
shapes and textures,
often discovered
that eggs or aubergines
went better, or leeks
or a plate of string beans.
A skull is so dominant.
It takes so much
bunched-up drapery,
such a ponderous
display of ornate cutlery,
just to make it
less prominent.

The greatest masters
preferred the
subtlest *vanitas,*
modestly trusting
to fruit baskets
to whisper
ashes to ashes,
relying on the
poignant exactness
of oranges to release
like a citrus mist
the always fresh fact
of how hard we resist
how briefly we're pleased.

GREAT THOUGHTS

Great thoughts
do not nourish
small thoughts
as parents do children.

Like the eucalyptus,
they make the soil
beneath them barren.

Standing in a
grove of them
is hideous.

TEST

Imagine a surface
so still and vast
that it could test
exactly what
is set in motion
when a single stone
is cast into its ocean.
Possessed of a calm
so far superior
to people's, it alone
could be assessed
ideally irascible.
In such a case,
if ripples yawed
or circles wobbled
in their orbits
like spun plates,
it would be the *law*
and not so personal
that what drops warps
and what warps dissipates.

CROWN

Too much rain
loosens trees.
In the hills giant oaks
fall upon their knees.
You can touch parts
you have no right to—
places only birds
should fly to.

ANGLES OF SUN

Only some
angles of sun
can grow corn,
which must be
drawn up by heat.
Where it is
barely warm
no one even
wants to eat
that kind of
light-fattened kernel
packed tight
like feed-lot beef cattle.
When obliquely lit
people think *sweet,*
they delight
in the tentative,
the partial, the
dish of berries
whose purple
varies.

BAD DAY

Not every day
is a good day
for the elfin tailor.
Some days
the stolen cloth
reveals what it
was made for:
a handsome weskit
or the jerkin
of an elfin sailor.
Other days
the tailor
sees a jacket
in his mind
and sets about
to find the fabric.

But some days
neither the idea
nor the material
presents itself;
and these are
the hard days
for the tailor elf.

AMONG ENGLISH VERBS

Among English verbs
to die is oddest in its
eagerness to be *dead,*
immodest in its
haste to be told—
a verb alchemical
in the head:
one speck of its gold
and a whole life's lead.

LIME LIGHT

One can't work
by lime light.

A bowlful
right at
one's elbow

produces no
more than
a baleful
glow against
the kitchen table.

The fruit purveyor's
whole unstable
pyramid

doesn't equal
what daylight did.

WHY WE MUST STRUGGLE

If we have not struggled
as hard as we can
at our strongest
how will we sense
the shape of our losses
or know what sustains
us longest or name
what change costs us,
saying how strange
it is that one sector
of the self can step in
for another in trouble,
how loss activates
a latent double, how
we can feed
as upon nectar
upon need?

DROPS IN THE BUCKET

At first
each drop
makes its
own pock
against the tin.
In time
there is a
thin lacquer
which is
layered and
relayered
till there's
a quantity
of water
with its
own skin
and sense
of purpose,
shocked at
each new violation
of its surface.

THE JOB

Imagine that
the job were
so delicate
that you could
seldom—almost
never—remember
it. Impossible
work, really.
Like placing
pebbles exactly
where they were
already. The
steadiness it
takes . . . and
to what end?
It's so easy
to forget again.

CLOSELY WATCHED THINGS

A too closely watched flower
blossoms the wrong color.
Excess attention to the jonquil
turns it gentian. Flowers
need it tranquil to get
their hues right. Some
only open at midnight.

DUTCH

Much of life
is Dutch
one-digit
operations

in which
legions of
big robust
people crouch

behind
badly cracked
dike systems

attached
by the thumbs

their wide
balloon-pantsed rumps
up-ended to the
northern sun

while, back
in town, little
black-suspendered
tulip magnates
stride around.

CRASH

Slip is one
law of crash
among dozens.

There is also
shift—
moving a
granite lozenge
to the left
a little,
sending down
a cliff.

Also toggles:
the idle flip
that trips
the rails
trains travel.

No act
or refusal
to act, no
special grip
or triple lock
or brake stops

crash; crash
quickens
on resistance
like a legal system
out of Dickens.

GRAVITY

Weight is a gift
you can't simulate.
It is useless if
you take it on too late.
The post-pupid
butterfly looks stupid
walking with her wings.
Some are, some are not,
weight-bearing things.

CHEMISE

What would the self
disrobed look like,
the form undraped?
There is a flimsy cloth
we can't take off—
some last chemise
we can't escape—
a hope more intimate
than paint
to please.

DEFERRED SILENCE

There is a
deferred silence
which only follows
a deferred sound.
As when an oak falls
when no one is around.
The violence waits
for someone to approach
to have just stopped.
There is that ozone
freshness to the aftershock.

ATTENTION

As strong as
the suction cups
on the octopus
are the valves
of the attention.

If threatened
or pulled off
they leave welts
and pink rings

but also
can unstick
unfelt
from things.

FAILURE

Like slime
inside a
stagnant tank

its green
deepening
from lime
to emerald

a dank
but less
ephemeral
efflorescence

than success
is in general.

Matrigupta

of Ujjain, India, wrote a poem that so pleased Rajah Vicrama Ditya HE WAS GIVEN THE ENTIRE STATE OF KASHMIR. *The poet ruled Kashmir for five years* (*118–123*) AND THEN ABDICATED TO BECOME A RECLUSE.

—*Ripley's Believe It or Not!*

(What a Trojan horse)
thought Matrigupta,
rewarded for his verse
by Rajah Ditya
with one of the nicest
states in India.
(Why couldn't it
have been a gold watch
or an inscribed plate?
I'll never write again
at this rate.)

"I am too blessed,"
went the little thank-you
poem he had rehearsed,
but already his words
were getting reversed
and he said, "I am
blue tressed," which was
only the first indication
of how things were in Kashmir
before his abdication.

Weakness and Doubt

Weakness and doubt
are symbionts
famous throughout
the fungal orders,
which admire pallors,
rusts, grey talcums,
the whole palette
of dusts and powders
of the rot kingdom
and do not share
our kind's disgust
at dissolution,
following the
interplay of doubt
and weakness
as a robust
sort of business;
the way we
love construction,
they love hollowing.

FAILURE 2

There could be nutrients
in failure—
deep amendments
to the shallow soil
of wishes.
Think of the
dark and bitter
flavors of
black ales
and peasant loaves.
Think of licorices.
Think about
the tales of how
Indians put fishes
under corn plants.
Next time hope
relinquishes a form,
think about that.

WATER UNDER THE BRIDGE

That's water under
the bridge, we say,
siding with the bridge
and no wonder,
given the sloping ways
of water which
grows so grey
and oily, toiling
slowly downward,
its wide dented
slide ever onward;
we aren't demented.

Your Face Will Stick

However bland we all
begin when picked
from the common
stock of cherubim,
your face will stick.
There will be
a spot at which
you hear the click.
Your baby ears—
pink shells—will
prick, your look grow
pixieish or dour,
fixed upon the
inner notch or
catch you can't resist,
like clocks set up
to strike the hour.

SURVIVAL SKILLS

Here is the virtue
in not looking up:
you will be the one
who finds the overhang
out of the sun
and something for a cup.
You will rethink meat;
you will know you have
to eat and will eat.
Despair and hope you keep
remote. You will not
think much about the boat
that sank or other boats.
When you can, you sleep.
You can go on nearly forever.
If you ever are delivered
you are not delivered.
You know now, you were
always a survivor.

AND ALL BECOMES AS BEFORE

—The Legend of the Baal-Shem,
             Martin Buber

So why do we want to go
if this travel is
so without profit

if not even a souvenir pebble
lodges in a boot waffle

or a half ticket sticks
in the corner of a pocket

if it is so perfect
that it takes every tick
of its private clock back

patting us down at the exit
like a bank dick

pushing us back into traffic?

Two More, and Up Goes the Donkey

An old cry at fairs, the showman having promised his credulous hearers that as soon as enough pennies are collected his donkey will balance himself on the top of a pole or ladder. Always a matter of "two more pennies," the trick is never performed.

—Brewer's Dictionary of Phrase and Fable

Old men
who were boys then
continue to imagine
how it would have been
to see a donkey
balancing above them.
Some see all four
small hooves
compressed on
the post top;
some see one.
It depends upon
which penny
wasn't spent,
which trick
wasn't done.

THE CATCH

Among nets
some are stout
and cast by
rubber-clad
sailors who
venture out
in boats and
talk of knots
and floats and
diesels and
gruesome accidents
to decent people.
Whereas the
nets approached
by birds and moths
and set by
Nabokovs in white
are lighter stuff
tied by threads
to branches
as though for sport.
. . .

A bird catches
like a shuttlecock.
In both events
what they get
only partly matches
what they sought
plus the problem
of the innocents.
One can admire
the common sense
it makes for sailors
who desire the
hardest, the most
backbreaking work,
the way you're tired
and broken to dispatch
by the time it's time
to justify the catch.